A Crocodile Grows Up

by Amanda Doering Tourville ~ illustrated by Michael Denman and William J. Huiett

Special thanks to our advisers for their expertise:

Zoological Society of San Diego
San Diego Zoo
San Diego, California

Susan Kesselring, M.A., Literacy Educator
Rosemount–Apple Valley–Eagan (Minnesota) School District

Editor: Christianne Jones
Designers: Angela Kilmer and Abbey Fitzgerald
Page Production: Melissa Kes
Art Director: Nathan Gassman
The illustrations in this book were created with acrylic.

Picture Window Books
151 Good Counsel Drive
P.O. Box 669
Mankato, MN 56002-0669
877-845-8392
www.picturewindowbooks.com

Library of Congress Cataloging-in-Publication Data
Doering Tourville, Amanda, 1980-
A crocodile grows up / by Amanda Doering Tourville ;
illustrated by Michael Denman & William J. Huiett.
p. cm. — (Wild animals)
Includes bibliographical references and index.
ISBN-13: 978-1-4048-3157-5 (library binding)
ISBN-13: 978-1-4048-3563-4 (paperback)
1. Crocodiles—Infancy—Juvenile literature. 2. Crocodiles—Development—Juvenile
literature. I. Denman, Michael, ill. II. Huiett, William J., 1943- ill. III. Title.
QL666.C925D64 2007
597.98'139—dc22   2006027304

Welcome to the world of wild animals! Follow a young Nile crocodile as she grows up along an African river. Watch as the tiny croc turns into one of the largest reptiles on Earth.

3

A high-pitched chirp comes from the ground.
A young crocodile is calling for her mother.

The young croc struggles out of her shell. She is surrounded by her brothers and sisters in a nest covered with dirt and sand.

The average female croc lays about 50 eggs at a time. This means the little croc may have 49 siblings!

5

The tiny croc hears scratching above her. Light fills the nest as the sand and dirt is kicked away. The young crocodile comes face to face with her enormous mother.

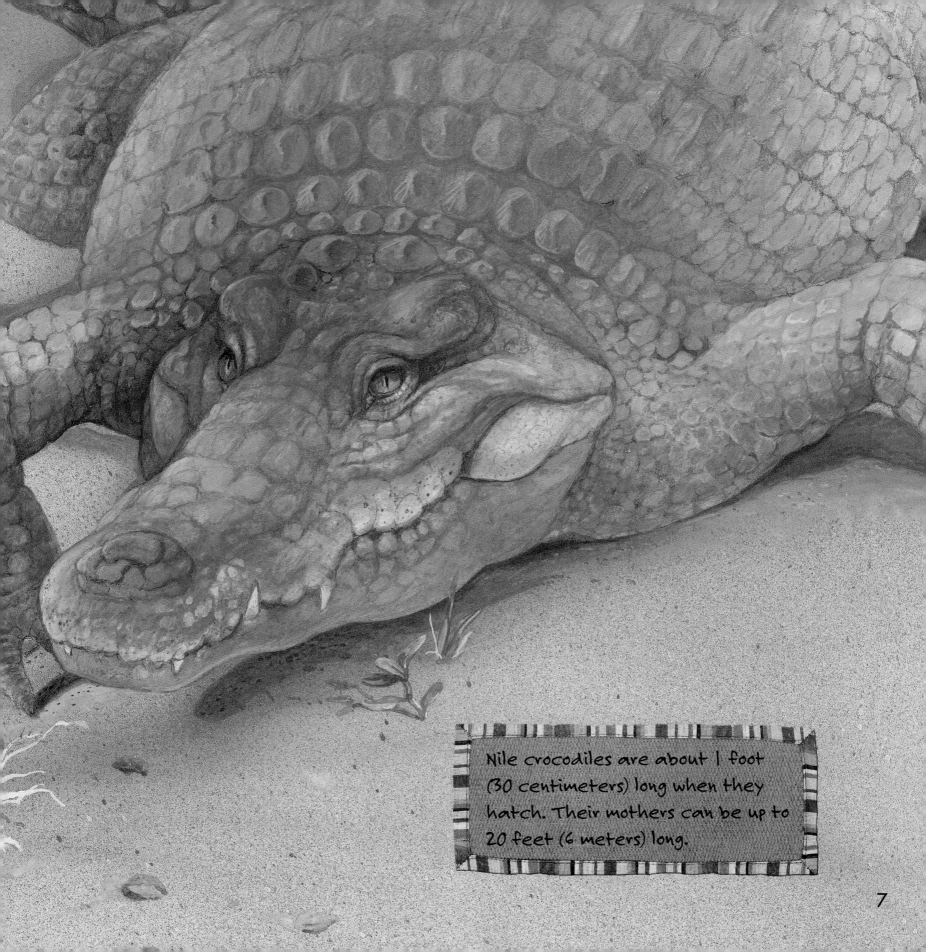

Nile crocodiles are about 1 foot (30 centimeters) long when they hatch. Their mothers can be up to 20 feet (6 meters) long.

7

Some of the young croc's siblings are still in their eggs. Their mother picks up the eggs with her huge jaws. She gently rolls the eggs between her tongue and the roof of her mouth to release the tiny crocodiles inside.

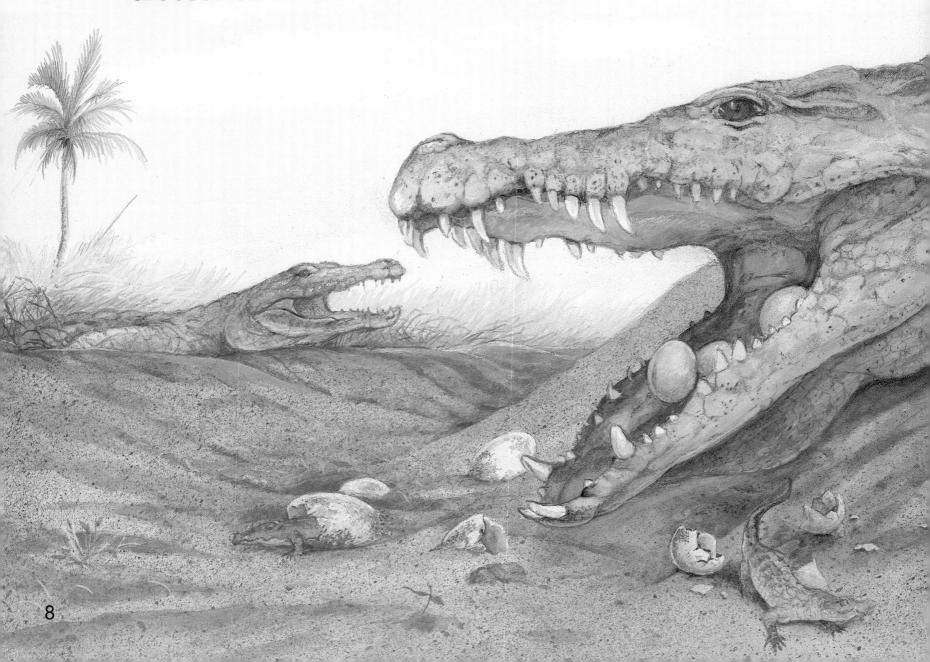

Crocodile mothers stay close to their nests for three months until their eggs hatch. They don't even leave the nest to eat.

The mother puts the newly hatched crocodiles into her mouth. One at a time, she safely carries each one to water. It is time for the crocodiles' first swimming lesson.

A crocodile stays near water its entire life.

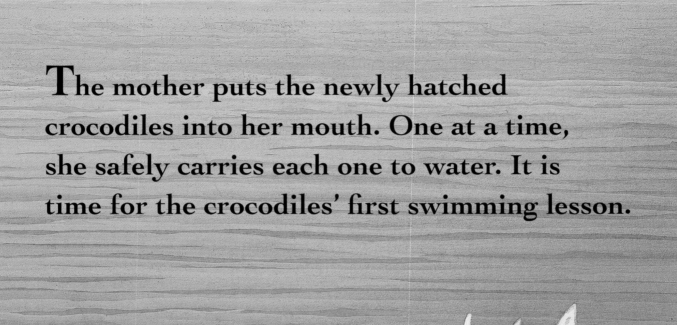

10

At the river, the mother opens her mouth. The young croc climbs out. She paddles into the water.

The young crocodile swims with her siblings but stays close to mom. The mother protects her young from other crocodiles and lizards that might want to eat them.

Even though their mothers try to protect them, many young crocodiles are eaten by predators.

13

The young crocodile is two months old. She still stays close to mom but likes diving and swimming.

On a dive, she sees a small fish and snaps it up. As she gets bigger, she will find more and more to eat.

Young crocodiles eat insects, worms, and small fish. Adult crocodiles eat just about anything they can catch, including larger fish, birds, other crocodiles, and lions.

15

At one year old, the young crocodile has doubled in size. She still sees her mother, but spends much of her time with other young female crocodiles.

A group of young female crocodiles is called a crèche.

The young crocodile is now two years old. She no longer depends on her mother. She must rely on the safety of her female group.

When her young are about two years old, the mother will no longer protect them.

18

The growing croc is almost 4 feet (1.2 m) long. Now small fish are just a snack. The young crocodile eats frogs, small birds, and larger fish.

The young croc spends many years on her own. She is now 10 years old and ready to become a mother. After mating, she digs a nest and lays her first eggs. She lies in the sun and watches over the nest.

She will be a good mother and protect her young like her mother protected her.

At 10 years old, the crocodile is about 7 feet (2.1 m) long. She will continue to grow for several more years.

21

Nile Crocodile Diagram

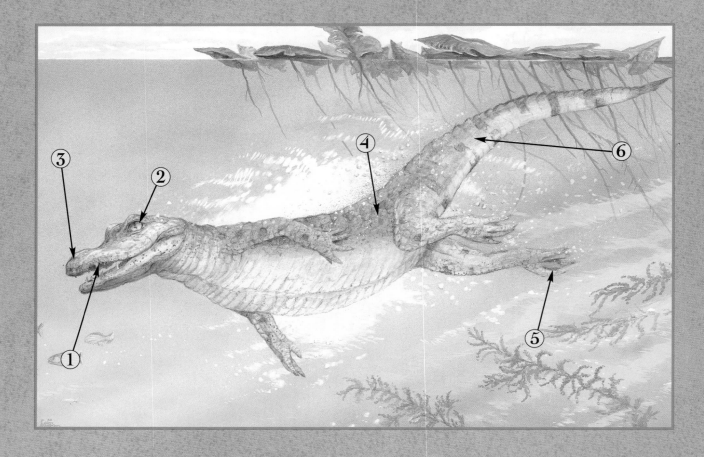

① TEETH A crocodile uses its sharp teeth to catch and hold prey.

② EYES A crocodile has good eyesight. When trying to catch prey, it swims with just its eyes and snout visible above the water to avoid being seen.

③ NOSTRILS A crocodile's nostrils are on the top of its snout. This way, the crocodile can breathe while the rest of its body is under the water.

④ SKIN A crocodile has thick, tough skin covered with scales and bony plates. Its dark skin blends in with muddy rivers and lakes.

⑤ FEET A crocodile's front feet have claws for gripping prey. Their back feet are webbed like a duck's feet.

⑥ TAIL A crocodile uses its tail to swim. The tail moves back and forth in an "S" shape to push the croc through the water.

22

Map

There are 23 types of crocodiles. The crocodiles in this book are Nile crocodiles. They live along the lakes and rivers of Africa.

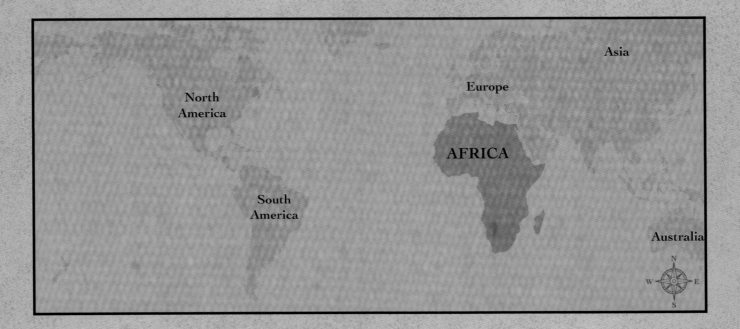

Glossary

chirp—a short, sharp sound a crocodile makes before it hatches

crèche—a group of young female crocodiles

hatch—to break out of an egg

predator—an animal that hunts and eats other animals

prey—an animal that is hunted and eaten for food

reptile—a cold-blooded animal with a backbone and scales

siblings—brothers and sisters

snout—the long front part of an animal's head that includes its nose, jaws, and mouth

To Learn More

At the Library

Bull, Schuyler. *Crocodile Crossing*. Norwalk, Conn.: Soundprints, 2003.
Llewellyn, Claire. *Crocodile*. Chanhassen, Minn.: Northword Press, 2004.
Murray, Julie. *Crocodiles*. Edina, Minn.: Abdo, 2005.

On the Web

FactHound offers a safe, fun way to find Web sites related to this book. All of the sites on FactHound have been researched by our staff.

1. Visit *www.facthound.com*
2. Type in this special code: 1404831576
3. Click on the FETCH IT button.

Your trusty FactHound will fetch the best sites for you!

Index

crèche, 17
eating, 14, 15, 19
eggs, 5, 8, 9, 20
eyes, 22
feet, 22
mating, 20
nest, 5, 6, 9, 20
nostrils, 22
predators, 13
prey, 22
skin, 22
snout, 22
swimming, 10, 12, 14, 22
tail, 22
teeth, 22

Look for all of the books in the Wild Animals series:

A Baboon Grows Up
A Crocodile Grows Up
An Elephant Grows Up
A Giraffe Grows Up
A Hippopotamus Grows Up

A Jaguar Grows Up
A Kangaroo Grows Up
A Lion Grows Up
A Rhinoceros Grows Up
A Tiger Grows Up

24